THE

GHOSTLY TALES

OF

MEMPHIS

For Eli and Vivian

Published by Arcadia Children's Books
A Division of Arcadia Publishing
Charleston, SC
www.arcadiapublishing.com

Spooky America is a trademark of Arcadia Publishing, Inc.

First published 2021

Manufactured in the United States

ISBN: 978-1-4671-9836-3

Library of Congress Control Number: 2021938351

Notice: The information in this book is true and complete to the best of our knowledge. It is offered without guarantee on the part of the author or Arcadia Publishing. The author and Arcadia Publishing disclaim all liability in connection with the use of this book.

All images courtesy of Shutterstock.com; p. 2 Sean Pavone/Shutterstock.com; p. 6 Tim Daugherty/Shutterstock.com; p. 20 Mont592/Shutterstock.com; p. 66 JustPixs/Shutterstock.com; p. 82 jdpphoto/Shutterstock.com.

THE GHOSTLY TALES OF MEMPHIS

LAURA CUNNINGHAM

Adapted from *Haunted Memphis* by Laura Cunningham

arcadia®
CHILDREN'S BOOKS

TABLE OF CONTENTS & MAP KEY

Beale Street, Memphis

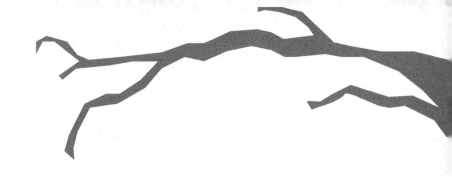

Introduction

The city of Memphis sits high on a bluff overlooking the Mississippi River. Memphis is known for great barbecue and for being the Home of the Blues and the Birthplace of Rock 'n Roll. But our city is also filled with tales of shadowy spirits lurking among us. Here, you will find stories of murder, disaster, tragedy, and more. The stories you will read about in this book are real. Some names have been changed to protect the identities of those who found themselves in the presence of the unexplainable. Are ghosts responsible for these otherworldly events? Maybe. Maybe not. I will leave that for you to decide. Join me as we pull back the veil separating the living from the dead, as we dig into Memphis's dark

past and enter the world of its spirits. Do you believe in ghosts? Have you ever come face to face with one? Have you heard things go bump in the night? Do you like to be scared? If so, this book is for you.

Fountain in Court Square

Court Square

When the founders of Memphis designed the city, they set aside a small piece of land to build a courthouse. They called this area Court Square. For whatever reason, though, nobody ever built a courthouse there, and it became a little park in a busy area of downtown Memphis.

Everyone loved spending time in Court Square. It was always filled with people enjoying themselves and was one of the most popular places in the city. Not long after the American Civil War, a group of important Memphians thought it would be a wonderful idea to add a beautiful fountain for everyone to enjoy in the center of the square. The group donated money to build the fountain, which

had a statue of the Greek goddess of youth, Hebe, at the center. Everyone loved the new fountain. The base was filled with deep water and was sometimes even stocked with fish.

One hot day in August, a ten-year-old boy named Claude Pugh went to the square to play and maybe do some work. Even though Claude was only ten years old, he had a job selling newspapers. His father had died, and his mother was so proud of him for helping their family.

The park was very busy that day. So many people were outside enjoying the summer air. Claude sat down on the rocks at the edge of the fountain and placed his small toy boat into the pool of water. Nobody is sure what happened next, but somehow Claude fell into the water. He was terrified—he could not swim! He struggled to touch the bottom of the fountain, but it was too deep. He grabbed at the rocks on the side, but they were too slippery and wet from algae and water. Worst of all, the square was filled with people that day, and not a single person tried to help poor Claude. A fireman came to the fountain, and it took him fifteen minutes to pull Claude from the water, but it was too late.

Claude's remains were buried at Elmwood Cemetery, yet even though Claude died over a hundred years ago, some say he never left Court Square. The Hebe fountain still stands there, but it is now much safer. The base was filled in, so it is no longer so deep. A small fence surrounds the bottom, so nobody can climb into the fountain. People will bring items to the fountain, such as toy boats, balls, and even rubber ducks! The items are placed into the water and begin to float around the fountain as if someone was there and actually moving the items. You can say "Claude can you move the boat to me?" and the boat will immediately change directions and come toward you!

The fountain is also a popular spot for ghost hunters. They bring equipment with them to communicate with the spirit of Claude. Investigators often use tools such as video and audio recorders to capture evidence of the paranormal. An electromagnetic field (EMF) detector is also commonly used for communicating with spirits. It's a really fancy name for a gadget that is very easy to use: the detector measures the strength of nearby electromagnetic fields, and different colored lights will flash depending on the level of energy it detects. If there is weak energy, the detector will flash green. A stronger energy field will flash red. Ghost hunters believe spirits can communicate by using paranormal energy to turn the light red in response to a question. For example, an investigator might say "Claude, are you here with us?" And if he is, then the detector will flash red.

On one tour, the guide brought an EMF detector and placed it on the ledge of the fountain. As she talked about Claude's sad and tragic death, something astounding happened. The EMF flew off the fountain and landed on the ground. The guide's hands were nowhere near it. Imagine everyone's shock when that happened. The group could not believe their eyes!

We may never know for sure if Claude is still here with us, but Memphians like to think he enjoys having visitors and is at peace playing at the fountain. Hopefully, he knows he will never be forgotten.

Overton Park

Overton Park is one of the largest parks in Memphis and one of the most popular places in the city. Hiking trails, an awesome playground, an amphitheater where really cool bands perform, and much more can be found at the park, including Rainbow Lake—a man-made lake built almost one hundred years ago.

Oh, we forgot to mention the ghosts. They have ghosts there, too.

Rainbow Lake was filled with all sorts of different colored electric lights. That's what gave the lake its name. It was the largest electric fountain in the country. The lake had sprays of water that would shoot almost twenty feet in the air. But the lights slowly stopped working, so they were replaced with flowers and trees instead.

One night, a young man named Chad decided to take his dog for a walk in Overton Park. The weather that evening was nice, and though he usually walked through the park two or three times a week, on this night, things seemed a little bit off to Chad. He did

not know exactly what was wrong, but he had a bad feeling that he could not shake. Everything seemed very still, no birds were chirping, and there was no wind rustling the leaves.

As he neared Rainbow Lake, his dog began to bark. Chad looked up, and there before him was a woman. She wore a light blue dress that seemed to be glowing. Her arms stretched out in front of her. She seemed to appear from out of nowhere.

"Miss, are you all right?" Chad asked. "Do you need any help?"

The woman took a few steps toward Chad but then disappeared just as fast as she had appeared. He could not believe his eyes and ran home with his dog as fast as he could. The next day, Chad told a friend about the mysterious woman.

"Hmm," his friend said. "One time I was in the park at night, and I saw blue flashes of light coming from the woods next to Rainbow Lake. I wonder—do you think it could be connected to the woman that you saw?"

After talking to a few other people, Chad found someone who knew a story about the mysterious woman. She had been seen walking around Rainbow Lake at night. She always looked like she was asking someone to help her. If anyone tried to get close to her, she vanished right in front of their eyes. Some people claimed to have even seen her rise up from the middle of the lake itself.

Others have seen streaks of blue light in the nearby woods and think it might possibly be the woman's trapped spirit. Some older Memphians remember hearing about a young woman who was attacked in the park, her body found in Rainbow Lake the next morning. Nobody knew her name, but she wore a blue dress, and her tragic murder remained unsolved. Perhaps the mysterious lady in blue is the ghost of the woman tossed in Rainbow Lake, unable to rest until she receives justice.

Worse yet, perhaps she is forever trapped, walking around the lake looking for someone to help her.

Memphis Zoo

The Memphis Zoo

The Memphis Zoo is one of the busiest and most popular zoos in the entire country. The zoo receives thousands of visitors every day, but many people believe the zoo becomes haunted at night.

A few years ago, the Edmondsons—a newly married couple—bought their dream home just down the street from the zoo. They loved their new house. The neighbors were all so friendly.

There was a police officer who lived a few houses down, so the couple always felt safe.

One night, not long after they had moved in, the couple was preparing to go upstairs to bed when they heard the loud "POP!" of a single gunshot piercing through the night air. Mrs. Edmondson looked at the clock above the fireplace. It was 9:15 p.m. Mr. Edmondson went and peered out the window. He did not see anyone, and nothing seemed out of place. The street was completely quiet and still. They decided to contact the police, just in case someone was hurt and needed help.

The next night, the Edmondsons were in their kitchen when they again heard the bang of a single gunshot. Mrs. Edmondson glanced over at the clock on the wall.

"That's strange," she said. "It's 9:15. It is the exact same time we heard that gunshot last night."

They went to the window and peered out. Again, nobody was outside and nothing appeared out of place. For the next week, the couple heard the same single gunshot each night at exactly 9:15 p.m.

On Saturday, the neighborhood gathered together for a cookout to welcome the new residents. The Edmondsons were excited to attend. They looked forward to meeting new people, plus the cookout would help get their minds off the odd nightly gunshot.

At 9:15, Mrs. Edmondson just happened to be talking to the police officer who lived on her street. And as if on cue, the single gunshot again rang out into the night. Mrs. Edmondson asked the officer if he knew why there was a gunshot at the same time each night. The officer's face became serious, and his voice dropped to just above a whisper.

He told her that every time the gunshot is reported, the police investigate and nothing out of the ordinary has been found.

"There is a sad tale that has been shared for several years now," the officer said.

Mrs. Edmondson listened as the officer went on to explain that many years ago, the director of the zoo lived in a house at the edge of the zoo property. Sadly, the wife of the former zoo director took her own life in the house. While her husband was in the kitchen preparing a meal, she went to the bedroom and killed herself with a single gunshot. The time was 9:15 p.m.

The director's house was eventually torn down and replaced with an area for children's rides. Zoo staff claim to have witnessed the ghost of the director's wife roaming the zoo late at night—often seen on the rides that have taken the place of her old home. New employees in the security department are even warned about her spirit's potential presence. It is believed she is forever trapped and not able to be at rest. Could she be tragically reliving her death over and over again, every night at the same time? I will leave that for you to decide.

Chickasaw Heritage Park and the Abandoned Marine Hospital

Chickasaw Heritage Park is a small park that overlooks the Mississippi River. The park was built on the site of an old Native American village called Chisca, which was also the name of the village leader. Two giant mounds of earth at the park are all that remain of the village. Many Native Americans consider the land to be sacred.

Eventually, a fort was built on that same land. During the American Civil War, soldiers disturbed the sacred land and dug a huge hole in one of the mounds. They used the hole to store weapons and ammunition. You can still see a small brick doorway on the side of the mound that led to the inside. There's something very strange about this small doorway. Every time someone paves it with bricks, someone or *something* comes along and pushes the bricks out. No matter how many times it's repaired, the bricks still fall out. It seems as if someone was mad the sacred land was disturbed and has tried to destroy the doorway. It's almost a guarantee that if you go to the park right now, there will be bricks knocked out of place.

Across the street from the park sits the old abandoned Marine Hospital. It is often called the most haunted location in Memphis. This is probably due to the thousands and thousands of deaths that occurred on the property. Soldiers weren't the only ones treated at the

hospital. During the 1800s, a highly contagious virus spread quickly throughout Memphis. This gruesome disease was called yellow fever, and it nearly wiped out the whole city. The symptoms of yellow fever were horrific and straight out of a nightmare. The hospital worked nonstop treating those who contracted the disease. When a patient died, their body was sent to the morgue in the basement. It took time to carry a body down several flights of stairs, so they came up with a faster way to move bodies. They built a chute—a slide that connected the upper floors down to the morgue in the basement. A body was put in the chute and would land at the bottom. It made removing dead bodies so much faster. But the chute was never cleaned and soon became so gory and gruesome, they began calling it "the Bloody Chute." Soon, people were dying faster than they could be buried, and there was no choice but to start piling the rotting, oozing dead bodies in the hospital's hallways. At some point, they buried some of the dead in the land across the street—the current location of Chickasaw Heritage Park! Nobody knows for sure just how many people are buried in the park or even what their names were.

With so many deaths, it is no wonder the hospital property is said to be haunted. There is a woman wearing a nurse's uniform who was often seen walking through the hospital grounds. It has been said she is the ghost of a nurse who treated yellow fever patients. She caught the disease herself and died a few days later. Maybe she is looking for patients to treat?

The hospital is a popular spot for ghost tours and investigations. A few years ago, a team of ghost hunters filmed an investigation of the hospital for a popular television show. There has often been unusual activity witnessed by people taking ghost tours.

One time, the tour guide pointed out an old-fashioned television that was turned on and could be seen in a window on the third floor. It was also common to see random lights on throughout the building. But here's the really creepy part. The electricity had been disconnected for years. It was not possible to turn a light on. Yet several people saw it with their own eyes. There were doors on the second- and third-floor balconies that would often open on their own. There were also windows that seemed to open on their own as well.

The French Fort neighborhood is located alongside the park and hospital property. Residents will tell you they do not like going out after dark. It seems like a ghostly spell falls on the neighborhood at dusk. Things feel strange outside, like something is not quite right. Some of the people who live in French Fort said they have seen the ghosts of the Native Americans, soldiers, and yellow fever victims wandering the area at night. And if you listen carefully, they can also be heard.

CHAPTER 5

The Haunted Carousel

Have you ever ridden on a carousel? How about a *haunted* carousel?

Well, there is something magical about the Grand Carousel. It is without a doubt one of Memphis's treasures. Generations of Memphians have fond memories of riding it, and it remains a favorite of residents young and old.

The Dentzel Carousel Company built the Grand Carousel in 1909. It originally operated at Forest Park in Chicago. A fire at the park caused significant damage to the ride, and it was returned to Dentzel to be repaired and refurbished. The carousel was then brought in 1923 to the Memphis Fairgrounds Amusement Park, where it remained for several decades.

The carousel was a work of art. It featured beautiful, bright-colored horses, mirrors,

clown heads, and more, all carved by hand. In the 1970s, a new amusement park called Libertyland opened at the fairgrounds. Renovations were made, and the Grand Carousel became a featured attraction.

Not long after Libertyland opened, stories circulated claiming the historic carousel was haunted by the ghost of a kind elderly employee whose spirit could be seen working on the ride late at night after the park closed. Sadly, this employee's life story was one of tragedy.

One day, a child was riding on the carousel and accidentally let go of the balloon he was holding. The balloon floated up and became trapped at the top of the ride. The kind ride operator went to retrieve the balloon and somehow became trapped in the carousel's gears, which caused his death. Years later, many claimed to still see his spirit throughout the park. Perhaps the kind employee was continuing to make sure the rides were safe, even after his death.

Libertyland closed its doors in 2005, and there was talk of the carousel being sold along with other rides from the park. However, a group of supporters came to the rescue! They successfully stopped the carousel from being sold. The carousel was dismantled and put into storage for protection. For a long time, it seemed like the public would never see the carousel again. It stayed in storage for several years while preparations were made to restore

the ride to its original glory. Newly restored, the Grand Carousel now resides at its newest home: the Children's Museum of Memphis.

Now that you know a little bit about the Grand Carousel's history, let's get back to the ghost story. Have you ever played the telephone game? Players form a line, and the first player comes up with a message and whispers it into the ear of the second person in the line. The second player repeats the message to the third player, and so on. By the time the message makes it to the last player, it is an entirely new message altogether.

When a ghost story gets shared, parts of it change over time. Details are added or removed, and the story you are left with may not even be close to the original. The ghost story of the haunted carousel and amusement park reminds me of the telephone game. You see, there actually was a tragic accident on the carousel involving an employee's death. Over time, the story was shared and changed, becoming the legend we know today.

The devastating accident took place about two months after Libertyland opened. A teenage employee, the assistant carousel operator,

died after getting caught in the ride's main gear. Investigators determined the young man had climbed up four feet on a stepladder, and his clothing became caught in the gears. No one ever determined why the employee was on the ladder near the gears. One theory a police officer suggested was that the employee tried to reach a balloon that had escaped from a small child riding the carousel. No one will ever know for sure. Hopefully, the young man is at peace. And perhaps it is his spirit that is seen across the park, looking out for the safety of others.

The Ghost at
the Corner

Here's the thing about ghosts: they make their own schedule. You usually have no idea when or where a ghost might appear. Most of the time, ghosts are unreliable and unpredictable.

And that is what makes this story so unique. This apparition was seen by dozens and dozens of witnesses. It is also remarkable because the events took place so long ago. This tale was shared by locals and passed down through generations. This is the story of the ghost at the corner.

At the corner of Chelsea Avenue and Sixth Street stands a Memphis landmark known simply as the "Old Brick Church." The first church members started building the church in 1856. That was over 150 years ago! As I mentioned earlier, ghosts are usually not predictable. However, in August 1889, this was not the case.

That summer, a young woman appeared outside the Old Brick Church at the corner of Chelsea and Sixth. The woman appeared late at night (or you could call it early morning)— at exactly 2:30 a.m. Several people noticed her, and soon rumors began to spread through the community. Night after night, the young woman appeared at the church on the corner. Neighbors speculated and gossiped about her. Who was she? Why was she there? The locals loved to speculate and make assumptions about the young lady. But they continued to leave her alone, and nobody tried to talk to her.

The mysterious woman appeared to be about twenty years old. She was tall and thin, with long, flowing red hair. She wore a long white robe with a black ribbon tied around her waist.

Before long, residents began to grow tired of seeing the mystifying woman every night. Some young men began to joke about her between friends. They passed her at the corner, saying things like, "Look! It's your girlfriend!" But eventually, the neighborhood lost interest in the woman, and they just left her alone. Well, not everyone left her alone.

One group of young men decided they had enough of the mystery. It was time to find out who she was and why she stood at the corner at such a late hour. One evening, they slowly approached her as she quietly stood at the corner. They slowly walked closer and closer until they were within just a few feet of her. Suddenly, the woman turned and walked to the side door of the church, and then she vanished! The bewildered men were stunned. She had simply disappeared right in front of them. The men checked the church door and found it locked. They all headed home, unable to make sense of what they saw. Over the next two nights, the men returned and met the same outcome. The mysterious woman went directly to the church door on Sixth Street and then disappeared.

Word began to spread across the community about the woman's new ability to disappear. Each night, groups as large as a dozen people showed up at the corner and attempted to capture the apparition. At this point, Memphians were certain she must be a ghost, but try as they might, no one could catch her. She was just too fast for them. Even the police tried to catch her, but they were also unsuccessful.

Finally, one young man came up with a plan. He would wait for the ghost at the door instead of chasing her from the street. That night, he arrived at the church at exactly 2:28, two minutes before she was expected to appear. He stood in position, blocking the church door. He knew if the ghost made her appearance and kept her usual routine, she would be forced to come in contact with him. He waited nervously, glancing up and down the street. He was alone, except for an old dog, sleeping peacefully on a nearby front porch. He gripped his pocket watch tightly. He was practically shaking with anticipation as he watched the minute hand click to 2:30. He quickly glanced up, and there, standing at the corner, the young woman appeared as if by magic. The moonlight bounced off her white gown, and she appeared to have a soft glow around her. The young man watched and waited for any slight movement. But she seemed content to stare mournfully into the darkness of night. Finally, the young man coughed loudly to get the woman's attention. Then he called to her to come to him. The woman immediately turned and quickly walked straight toward him. When she was within feet of him, she lifted her head. Until now, no one had fully seen the woman's face.

The man gasped in horror upon seeing her. Her expression was that of despair. She had large, sunken black eyes, and her bony face terrified him. The ghostly woman reached her arms out toward the man, attempting to embrace him. He reached out to embrace her in return but soon realized he had not touched her. She had actually passed right through him! He turned around and looked at her, heading straight to the door.

But this time, she turned back one last time and stared directly into the frightened man's eyes, and then she was gone.

The James Lee House

This tale is filled with all the elements of a good story. It's about a ghost who seeks revenge against the people who wronged her, and in this case, it is a story of family betrayal. Now, I am especially fond of this story and its ghostly main character. Want to know why? She and I both have the same name—Laura!

Our story begins at the James Lee House, located on Adams Avenue, in an area known as

Victorian Village. In the late 1800s, the street was nicknamed "Millionaires Row." Huge, beautiful mansions lined each side of the street, and in order to live on Adams Avenue, you had to be very wealthy.

In 1848, a lumberman named William Harsson began building a small farmhouse outside of the Memphis city limits on a piece of land that would later become the intersection of Orleans Street and Adams Avenue. However, the peaceful farmland Harrson dreamed of quickly became surrounded by large mansions in every direction.

Harsson had two daughters, Charlotte and Laura. In 1849, Laura married Charles Goyer, and the couple lived at the home alongside her sister and father. Charles was a businessman, and soon he had enough money to buy the house from Laura's father. Have you ever heard of the Union Planters Bank? There is a legend passed down that Charles Goyer became so wealthy, he created the Union Planters Bank just so he would have a place to store his money. Can you even imagine having that much money?

Meanwhile, the couple wanted a bigger home, so every few years, they built on more rooms, making their house larger and larger. Unfortunately, tragedy struck the young couple. Laura became sick with the deadly yellow fever virus and died just a few days later.

Now this is where the story takes a sharp turn: after Laura died, her husband, Charles, married her sister, Charlotte!

Years after Laura's death, Charles and Charlotte sold the home to the Lee family. The Lees remained in the house for several decades, and they eventually turned the home into an art school. Eventually, the art school moved out of the home, and the house stood vacant for over fifty years. A historical preservation group watched over the house and did repairs through the years. Finally, a couple purchased the home and restored it to its former glory, converting it into a bed-and-breakfast that is still open today.

For decades, the ghost of a woman in a red dress has been seen throughout the house. She often walks up and down the staircase. Ghost hunters investigated the mansion and reported sensing the presence of an angry female spirit. Workers making renovations to the house reported sensing movement in empty rooms throughout the house that were vacant. Students who attended the art school also regularly saw a woman on the staircase. She wore a red flowing dress and appeared to glide down the front staircase, then vanishing before their eyes. They called her the "Woman in Red." The Woman in Red was often seen in one of the oldest rooms in the house. She sits in a rocking chair, and they feel that she is very, very sad.

The theory is the Woman in Red is the ghost of Laura Goyer. She continues to return after death because she is worried about her children. Countless numbers of people have felt an angry presence coming from the house. The anger is so strong, some even say you can feel it all the way from the street outside! In addition to anger, some sense a sadness coming from the home. There are so many emotions coming from the house they believe Laura has actually never left. Her spirit is angry, hurt, and surrounded by sadness. She is unable to accept her death and cannot move forward to the afterlife.

While Laura's story is sad, there is still a ray of hope for Laura's spirit. On a tour, a guide began speaking softly to Laura. The guide gently told her that her children were okay and she never had to worry about them again. Immediately the group sensed a feeling of relief, as if Laura's pain and sadness had just lifted.

The *Sultana*

Did you know the deadliest boating disaster in US history took place on the Mississippi River just north of Memphis? The ship was the *Sultana*, and some people are convinced it still sails on the river. It would seem the vessel is still trying to make it to the next port safely, but it is forever doomed to constantly repeat its fateful journey—and its passengers are destined to never return home.

The *Sultana* was a steamboat that regularly traveled up and down the Mississippi River. The American Civil War was coming to an end, and released prisoners needed a way to travel back home. In Vicksburg, the captain of the *Sultana* was offered a large amount of money to have prisoners board his ship and then return them back to the North. The captain was paid a sum per prisoner, and that gave him an idea. He decided to fill the ship with as many people as it could possibly hold, as more passengers meant more money.

The *Sultana* was a small ship, and it was built to carry no more than 376 passengers. Unfortunately, the captain's greed led him to make a very poor decision. The ship set sail for the North with 2,137 people on board. Prisoners were practically standing on top of one another, as there was no room on the ship to even sit down.

Not long after leaving port, the ship started experiencing problems. It struggled as it made its way upriver, so when it reached Memphis, some repairs were made. But the overcrowded

steamboat continued on its journey into the middle of the night.

It was almost 2:00 a.m. when the ship's boilers suddenly exploded. The weight of the passengers was too much for the ship to withstand. Nearly everyone was killed, as many of the passengers died instantly from the explosion, and many others drowned after being thrust into the water. A handful of lucky men held on to any piece of debris they could find, but it took thirty minutes before the first rescue ship arrived. By then, what little was left of the *Sultana* had drifted deeper into the water before finally sinking a few hours later.

The disaster was horrific. Investigators determined 1,529 men died in the accident. In fact, more people died in the *Sultana* disaster than died on the *Titanic*. Hundreds upon hundreds of dead bodies floated down the Mississippi River. Some bodies were found months later, and some even drifted as far back as Vicksburg, where the doomed voyage began.

Sadly, the disaster was overlooked by the general public. Newspapers were focused on the assassination of President Abraham Lincoln in Washington, DC. His assassin, John Wilkes Booth, was captured the day before the *Sultana* accident. With the papers preoccupied with the events in Washington, DC, the *Sultana* tragedy was soon forgotten.

That said, there have been numerous reports of people having terrifying experiences on the river. I spoke about it with a barge captain, Truman Morrison. As he told me his experience, I could tell he was terrified just thinking about it. One night, as he was on the river approaching Memphis, he noticed a murky, swirling mist beginning to form across the water. The air felt hot as the mist began transforming into a steamy fog. It was so heavy, it became impossible to see. Then the fog began changing to a glowing red color. As the fog became redder and redder, the air began to get hotter and hotter. Then Morrison heard the screams. They sounded like nothing on this earth he had heard before, as though someone

were crying out in horrible pain. The screams grew louder and louder, and then, suddenly, they stopped. Morrison watched as the red light disappeared and the heavy fog dissolved.

There was no doubt in Morrison's mind that he had witnessed something otherworldly, and he was certain he'd experienced the energy created from the *Sultana* tragedy. He's not the only one who experienced the terrifying fog, by the way. Many residents who live on the bluffs overlooking the river have seen it, too. They all say it was a devastating experience they will not soon forget.

The Orpheum Theater

The Orpheum Theater

If you were to ask any Memphian "What is the most haunted place in Memphis?" they will tell you it is absolutely the Orpheum Theater. They could also probably tell you the name of the Orpheum's most popular ghost, Mary.

The Orpheum Theater is located at the corner of Main Street and Beale Street. There has always been a theater at that spot, even back in the 1800s. But keep in mind: movies and television did not exist back then, so watching plays and performances at the theater was one of the most popular forms of entertainment. Everyone enjoyed going to the theater. But back then, all the theaters in the city were rather small. As the city grew, however, a group of Memphis businessmen came together and decided Memphis deserved to have a nice theater. So they built the Grand Opera House on that corner, and it was one of the finest theaters in the entire county. But as the years went by, fewer and fewer people went to the theater. The Grand Opera House lost a lot of money, so a new company took control of the theater in order to keep it open. It renamed the building the Orpheum.

The theater had been open for around thirty years when a tragedy occurred. No one knew how it happened, but a small fire broke out in the back of the building. The fire spread quickly ,and within minutes, the entire theater was consumed with flames. The building was destroyed. All that was left were ashes and soot. So the owner decided to build a new theater with a different design. This new Orpheum Theater is the structure that still stands today.

The new Orpheum closed in 1940. People didn't really go to plays anymore. Movies were now the most popular form of entertainment. So the Malco Theatre Corporation purchased the building and turned it into a movie theater. It was a popular entertainment spot for several years. But as movies grew in popularity, more and more movie theaters were built around the city. It seemed like every neighborhood had its own little movie theater. Fewer and fewer people were going downtown. Why would they drive all the way downtown when they could just go to the theater down the street? And so when the movie theater closed, the building was turned back into the Orpheum. Just like it used to be and still is today.

Remember how I said earlier that everyone thought the Orpheum was the most haunted place in the city? Well, I have a theory why that is probably correct. For over one hundred years, Memphians went to that corner to be entertained. And they looked forward to going to the performances. Just imagine, a theater filled with different types of people from throughout the community, all coming together for the same reason: to be entertained and enjoy the entire experience. People were always happy when they were at the theater. It only makes sense that a lost ghost would want to be there. And a theater is always busy. Even on days without a performance, the building would be filled with people behind the scenes preparing for the next performance. A lonely ghost might want to stay in the theater permanently. That way they would never be alone.

Almost fifty years ago, a paranormal group conducted a detailed investigation of the theater. At the time, they determined there were seven distinct spirits who called the Orpheum their home. That was fifty years ago. Can you imagine how many more there are now? One of those spirits was Mary. She is the ghost most Memphians know haunts the Orpheum. Mary is the ghost of a young girl who has been seen roaming the theater's hallways for over one hundred years.

If you remember, the Orpheum was a movie theater for a few decades. During that time, the management told the employees to not talk about the ghosts they saw or the stories they heard. If anybody asked, they were to respond by saying something like, "No, the theater is absolutely not haunted." The movie theater's managers thought it would be bad for business if people thought the building was haunted. For a very long time, Mary was often seen at the theater, but only the employees knew about her. Her presence was hidden from the general public.

When the movie theater finally closed, the new managers no longer kept Mary a secret. If anyone asked if the Orpheum was haunted, they were told stories about the times Mary made herself known. Everyone who saw Mary always described her the same way.

She looked like she was around twelve years old. She had long brown hair that she wore in pigtails. Her white outfit looked like it may have been her school uniform. She wore black stockings, and there were no shoes on her feet. People have seen her in all areas of the building. But she is most often seen in seat C-5 on the balcony overlooking the stage. The staff refer to it as "Mary's favorite seat," and they don't sell a ticket for it. They leave it open just for Mary.

The Guardian Dog's Ghost

The story of the guardian dog's ghost may be the oldest ghost story in Memphis. It dates back before Memphis even became a city. This story took place even before the European explorers set eyes on the Mississippi River. On a dark night in early winter, you can stand on the bluff overlooking the river. If you listen carefully to the wind, you might hear an eerie howl piercing the night air. It is the sorrowful cry of an unearthly animal. Fishermen have often heard the cry. Those who lived along the bluff have heard it, too. According to legend, this is the wail of the guardian dog's ghost. Some say when you hear the dog, it is a warning that danger is close.

The story of the guardian dog comes from an old Chickasaw legend. A long time ago, two now-separate Native American tribes, the Chickasaw and the Choctaw, were once part of a large, single tribe. They lived happily and peacefully on land in the far West. After many years, some tribal members wanted to leave and search for new lands to settle. The group who wanted to leave grew in size to nearly 30,000 tribe members. While they were preparing for their journey, a medicine man gave the group two charms. These gifts were to guide and protect them along their journey. The first gift was a large white dog. This dog's duty was to warn the people of any danger they might encounter on their path. The medicine man's second gift was a tall, red pole. They called this pole the sanctified rod.

The tribe soon went on their way, not knowing where they were destined to find their

new home. They walked during the day and stopped to rest at night. Every night, the tribe's chief performed a ceremony to determine where the tribe would go next. He planted the sanctified rod firmly into the ground. In the morning, they would find the rod leaning. The tribe would then travel in the direction the rod was leaning. Without fail, the large white dog stood at the front of the group, leading the way. Night after night, the chief planted the rod. Every morning, the rod leaned toward the east. Days turned into weeks, and weeks turned into months. Every day, they continued walking east, with the white dog leading the way.

Eventually, the tribe reached the largest river they had ever seen, the river now known as the mighty Mississippi. The tribe camped on the river's west bank for many days, determining the best way to cross. It would take enormous preparation to get thousands of people and all the supplies safely across the river. They began by building rafts with driftwood and area trees.

Finally, the day came, and they were ready to cross. The white dog began barking and acting very strange. He ran around nudging at the rafts and whimpering. No one had ever seen him act this way. Still, they knew the voyage would be dangerous no matter how well they had prepared, so they moved forward on their journey.

Tragically, a storm rolled in not long after they began the crossing. The winds blew strong, and the rain was heavy. All across the river, people tried to stay afloat. Sadly, hundreds drowned in the storm. Several rafts carrying much-needed supplies overturned. The raft carrying the white dog

was also destroyed. For the survivors, the loss of the dog was devastating. He helped maintain morale throughout the long, tiresome journey, and his absence was felt by everyone who managed to live.

The grief-stricken travelers camped on the river bluff following the storm. That night, the chief conducted the usual ceremony, placing the rod into the ground. In the morning, the tribe woke to a great surprise. When the chief went to the sanctified rod, he found it standing straight, just as it was the night before. This had never happened. The tribe did not travel that day. Instead, they decided to hold a meeting and discuss what they should do next. That night, the tribe's elders met and concluded the sanctified rod was giving them a sign. They believed it was a sign to settle nearby on the bluff. However, not all elders agreed on the pole's symbolism. This disagreement caused a separation among the tribal members. One chief, Chief Chickasaw, decided he and his followers would obey the action of the gods and settle on the bluffs. A second chief, Chief Choctaw, had a different opinion. He thought they should head toward the south. The two groups divided and became the separate Chickasaw and Choctaw tribes we know today.

However, some say the ghost of the white dog still roams the banks of the Mississippi River trying to warn and protect people. So if you see or hear him, just be careful, for danger lies close by.

WELCOME

WOODRUFF FONTAINE
HOUSE MUSEUM

ENTRANCE

MUSEUM PARKING LOCATED BEHIND
MANSION OFF WASHINGTON AVE

Woodruff-Fontaine House Museum

The Woodruff-Fontaine House

When a house is haunted, it is common for people to see ghosts or shadowy figures. They may also hear the ghosts knocking on doors or creaking across floors. Some people even feel a ghostly presence from a sudden drop in temperature, sending a chill down their spine. But did you know some people have actually *smelled* a ghost? It's true! In Memphis, visitors to the Woodruff-Fontaine House Museum often smell a flowery fragrance, like an old-fashioned perfume. They also smell cigar smoke drifting down from the third floor. The museum guides are very familiar with these ghostly smells. Visitors to the museum report experiencing them on a regular basis.

The Woodruff-Fontaine House Museum is located in Victorian Village on Adams Avenue. The house is the former home of the Woodruff and, later, the Fontaine families. In 1870, Amos Woodruff, a carriage maker from New Jersey, moved to Memphis to expand his growing business. He soon began construction on a large, ornate mansion for his wife, Phoebe, and their four children. Woodruff wanted his house to be one of the finest in the city, perhaps one of the finest in the entire South! He hired only the most talented professionals to design his home, and he used only the finest-quality materials to build it. He carefully designed even the smallest of details. For example, each brick was made by hand.

Woodruff became very successful in Memphis. He became president of two banks and controlled several area companies. A few years after moving into their home on Adams Avenue, Woodruff's nineteen-year-old daughter Mollie married a man named Egbert Wooldridge. They held their wedding in the home's downstairs parlor. The wedding was a beautiful and joyous event.

Mollie and Egbert had no way of knowing they would only have a few short years of happiness together.

The young newlyweds decided to live in the mansion with Mollie's family. They turned several rooms on the second floor into their own private space. After they had been married for a few years, Mollie and Egbert found out they were going to have a baby. They were so excited. On a cold February day in 1875, Mollie gave birth to a little girl. Tragically, the baby died shortly after she was born. The entire family was just devastated. The young couple went into mourning. They wore black clothing and did not leave the house unless it was absolutely necessary.

After three months had passed, some of Egbert's friends thought he might feel better if he got out of the house. They planned a fishing trip along the Mississippi River. Mollie and Egbert both thought a fishing trip would be good for him. Mollie could even take in views of the river from the top window in the home's tower. For the first time in a long time, the couple had reason to smile.

On the morning of the fishing trip, Mollie kissed Egbert goodbye as he left with his friends. She settled down in the sewing room and worked on some of her projects. That afternoon, she was startled by a loud disturbance outside. She could hear men shouting but could not make out what they were saying. Then there was loud knocking at the front door. Mollie rushed downstairs to see who it was and what could possibly be going on outside. A group of men stood in the doorway.

They were carrying Egbert, and he did not look well.

The men quickly carried Egbert upstairs and into the bed. Someone sent for the doctor. There had been an accident during the fishing trip: Egbert had fallen into the river and swallowed quite a bit of water. The doctor determined Egbert had pneumonia and needed to rest. The family waited and hoped he would get better. Sadly, Egbert died three days later. He died in the same room as his daughter just three months before.

The widowed Mollie continued to live with her parents until she married her second

husband, a nice man named James Henning. They moved to a new home, and before long, Mollie was pregnant. But this child also died soon after birth, just like her daughter years before. Sadly, Mollie never had another child. In 1917, Mollie died at her sister's home from heart disease. She was only fifty-six years old.

Around the time Mollie married James Henning, Amos Woodruff sold the home to Noland Fontaine. The Fontaine family lived in the home for the next forty-six years. Noland Fontaine was one of the wealthiest cotton producers in the country. Raising eight children ensured the Fontaines' home became the scene of many elaborate parties, with prominent guests arriving from all around the country.

Noland Fontaine actually died in the first floor's parlor during a surgery. He had been having health problems, and the doctors were not sure why. One doctor, Dr. Taylor, agreed to operate on Fontaine to see if he could find out what was wrong. Dr. Taylor was married to Noland's daughter Molly. Noland's family watched the surgery. During the surgery, something terrifying happened. His son Elliot recorded the event in his journal. During the operation, Fontaine's heart stopped, and he appeared to be dead, when suddenly he sat up and said, "I have seen the devil. He's thirsty and asked me for a drink of water." Then he laid back down and was gone.

With time, Noland Fontaine's wife, Virginia, and his son Elliot also died in the home, and the Woodruff-Fontaine House and the James Lee House next door became an art school. When the art school moved to a new location, the homes became vacant and were frequently vandalized. Fortunately, a preservation group restored the house and turned it into a museum, which has been open for almost sixty years.

People believe Mollie Woodruff and Elliot Fontaine are the spirits that remain at the house, although there may be others. After Mollie Woodruff died in 1917, they believe she attached herself to her former home. The center of Mollie's activity is her old bedroom on the second floor, called the "Rose Room." That is the room where her daughter and husband both died. A hint of her flowery perfume drifts through the air. Students who lived in the house while attending the art school heard sighs and whispers coming from Mollie's old bedroom. During the house's restoration period, construction workers felt her presence, as if an unseen person walked behind them on the stairs. People often heard her footsteps on the stairs, along with slamming doors.

Visitors to the house have experienced paranormal activity year-round. But there is a noticeable, heightened sense of disturbance between February and May, possibly related to the time between the deaths of Mollie's daughter and husband. Some say they hear a baby crying and the light whisper of a woman's voice. On the day before the anniversary of Egbert's death, museum guides have heard the sound of a woman's muffled crying. Upon climbing the stairs to find the source, the crying stopped before they reached the first landing. Once back downstairs, the crying began again. Shutters flapping violently, chandeliers swinging, and doors slamming have also been witnessed. Lights have turned on after the museum was closed. There have been a few people who claimed to see Mollie herself. She wore a green dress and paced back and forth in her bedroom.

Now the home's second ghost, possibly Elliot Fontaine, resides on the third floor. Visitors often report smelling cigar smoke. While no one has physically seen the third-floor ghost, they have strongly sensed it is a man. Some people have said he is hostile and they felt threatened, while others have felt the exact opposite. One man felt the spirit was pleased to have him visit and was eager for him to stay.

The Hunt-Phelan Mansion

When you picture Beale Street, you imagine its blues clubs and late-night activity. But farther down, there were once stately mansions. The Hunt-Phelan House is the only one remaining. It is considered one of the most historic homes in the city. During the American Civil War, both the Northern and the Southern armies used it for headquarters. General Grant stayed there, and important battles were planned in the home's parlor. During the war, the house was used as a hospital, and later, it housed teachers sent to Memphis to educate freed slaves. At least five US presidents have stayed in the home. The house has been a museum and a bed-and-breakfast.

During the Civil War, seventeen soldiers died in the house during its time as a hospital. One of those soldiers was Private William McClintock. McClintock suffered a gunshot wound in his leg. The wound became infected, and his leg had to be amputated. He was in excruciating pain during the surgery, and he accidentally mentioned he was a spy. He was promptly taken to the backyard and hanged. The sound of a man hopping is often heard on the top floor of the mansion.

One popular legend dates back to one of the yellow fever epidemics in the 1870s. The Hunt family decided to leave Memphis as

soon as they heard the disease had reached the city. They gathered what they needed as quickly as possible. Thousands of Memphians were also fleeing the city, and it would soon

be impossible to find transportation out of town. Nathan Wilson was the family's most trusted servant. He would remain in the city to take care of the home and property while the family was away. The Hunts left Nathan with a chest full of gold to be used to take care of the estate's finances. Not long after the family left, Nathan became a victim of the fever. He lay in his bed and died a few days later. After Nathan passed away, the other servants noticed a pair of Nathan's boots were muddy and lying next to his bed. A muddy shovel was there, too.

Everyone searched for the chest of gold, but it was nowhere to be found. According to legend, Nathan buried the chest before he died. He wanted to keep it safe for when the family returned. But he died before telling anyone its location. But, at midnight during a full moon, if you stand in the middle of three trees (once located in the mansion's front yard), Nathan Wilson's ghost will appear and guide you directly to the lost treasure.

Elmwood Cemetery

13

Elmwood Cemetery

A collection of ghost stories would not be complete without a few tales from a cemetery, the perfect location for hauntings. Elmwood Cemetery is the oldest active cemetery in Memphis. It opened in 1852. The cemetery's name was chosen in a drawing. Several potential names were placed in a hat, and "Elmwood" was the name picked.

Elmwood was designed to look like a large park. It is eighty acres of rolling, wooded landscape. That is the size of eighty football fields! Currently, there are 70,000 people buried there. It is the final resting place for the famous, the infamous, and of course, ordinary people. War veterans, political leaders, spies, outlaws, and murderers are all buried there. People who never associated with one another in life are now located next to one another in death at Elmwood. With so many colorful characters buried there, it is no wonder Elmwood has its share of ghost stories.

Years ago, the cemetery caretaker first experienced Elmwood's spirits as he closed the cemetery for the evening, just around dusk. As he crossed the grounds, he noticed four men gathered at the tallest hill, located right in the center of the cemetery, known as Lenow Circle. The caretaker thought they must have entered the cemetery while he was busy closing some of the other gates. He noticed the men were dressed in some kind of odd costume. They were dressed completely in white. They had on white top hats and white suit jackets with long tails. As the caretaker approached the men, he

was shocked by what he saw. The men did not just walk away, they glided across the lawn and then disappeared. The entire encounter lasted no longer than a minute. The four men never seemed to notice the caretaker's presence.

Those who heard the caretaker's story believed they knew just who the four men were. They were David Park "Pappy" Hadden, Napoleon Hill, Henry A. Montgomery, and Archibald Wright—four well-known Memphis businessmen. When they were alive, they met every morning at the corner of Madison Avenue and Main Street. They met to discuss business and politics and to simply enjoy each other's company. It seemed like these four men carried their routine over into the afterlife. Other people besides the caretaker have also seen the men. They say they will appear at the top of the Lenow Circle hill each night at the stroke of midnight.

Elmwood's main office is a small building referred to as "the Cottage." It was the home for Elmwood's former superintendent. He lived in the house so he could be ready in case of any problems at the cemetery, day or night. They turned it into the official business office in 1897. They added a walk-in vault for the cemetery records and a small parlor for visitors. There is a ghost there who has a tendency to turn the water faucets on and off.

The ghost of Alice Mitchell also haunts the cemetery. Photographs taken of her gravesite often appear blurry and filled with orbs. In the late 1800s, Alice committed what became known as the crime of the century. She was a teenager who murdered another teenage girl, Frederica "Freda" Ward, in downtown Memphis in broad daylight and in front of hundreds of witnesses. Alice approached Freda with her father's shaving razor and slashed her throat. She calmly walked away as Freda dropped to the ground and died in the street. The murder trial fascinated the entire country. At the trial, Alice was found not guilty due to insanity. She was sent to a mental institution and died a few short years later. Although her death was reported as tuberculosis, many believed she killed herself by jumping into the water tower on the hospital's roof. Alice's grave is in direct view of Freda's grave. Freda is unable to escape her murderer, even in death.

Elmwood closes each day at dusk. It does hold occasional evening tours for the brave souls wishing to see the spirits come alive at night.

Laura Cunningham can trace her Memphis roots back six generations. She developed an interest in ghost stories and folklore while working in local museums and libraries. Sharing stories with her coworkers inspired her first book, *Haunted Memphis*. Her second book, *Lost Memphis*, was published the following year.

Laura is the mother of two amazing children, Eli and Vivian, born ten years apart. When she is not writing books about the history of Memphis, her interests include genealogy, DIY projects and a mild to moderate obsession with True Crime.

Check out some of the other Spooky America titles available now!

Spooky America was adapted from the creeptastic Haunted America series for adults. Haunted America explores historical haunts in cities and regions across America. Each book chronicles both the widely known and less-familiar history behind local ghosts and other unexplained mysteries. Here's more from author Laura Cunningham: